Controlling Men

*How to Cope with
and Transform Your
Controlling Husband
or Boyfriend*

by Luna Parker

Table of Contents

Introduction 1

Chapter 1: Is Your Husband / Boyfriend Controlling? 7

Chapter 2: Controlling Relationship: Work On It, Or Leave? 15

Chapter 3: Different Ways to Deal with and Transform a Controlling Husband / Boyfriend 25

Chapter 4: The Role of Counseling and Psychotherapy 33

Chapter 5: Calling It Quits: Healing and Transformation 37

Conclusion 45

Introduction

Marriages and relationships are a lot more successful if both parties are on the same page. But things can quickly go in the other direction if your husband or boyfriend becomes too controlling. Your partner is meant to share a life with you, dealing with the same difficulties and sorrows that you are. When this goes wrong though, they can be the one who's giving you the burden.

It is very important to draw a line if your boyfriend or husband's controlling behavior is suffocating you. There is no need to put up with the distress, especially if things are going overboard. It is important to remember that a man who is obsessed with controlling your life is enough to destroy even the strongest relationship, and the strongest person.

In this book, you will learn all the secrets to managing and transforming your man's controlling demeanor. Men can have a tendency to become controlling and dominant in a relationship, and these things make them hard to deal with at times. As a woman, you need to determine whether your partner is simply being proactive, or whether he has actually become unacceptably controlling. This will tell you what the next steps to take are. If you find that you are living with a controlling partner, this book will give you the means by which to overcome the problem and get back to a loving relationship.

Dealing with controlling men can be risky and complicated. However, this should not keep you from trying to save your relationship. It may be hard, but it is entirely possible to deal with this problem successfully.

Let's get started!

© Copyright 2014 by LCPublifish LLC - All rights reserved.

This document is geared towards providing reliable information in regards to the topic and issue covered. The publication is sold with the idea that the publisher is not required to render accounting, officially permitted, or otherwise, qualified services. If advice is necessary, legal or professional, a practiced individual in the profession should be ordered.

- From a Declaration of Principles which was accepted and approved equally by a Committee of the American Bar Association and a Committee of Publishers and Associations.

In no way is it legal to reproduce, duplicate, or transmit any part of this document in either electronic means or in printed format. Recording of this publication is strictly prohibited and any storage of this document is not allowed unless with written permission from the publisher. All rights reserved.

The information provided herein is stated to be truthful and consistent, in that any liability, in terms of inattention or otherwise, by any usage or abuse of any policies, processes, or directions contained within is solely and completely the responsibility of the recipient reader. Under no circumstances will any legal responsibility or blame be held against the publisher for any reparation, damages, or monetary loss due to the information herein, either directly or indirectly.

Respective authors own all copyrights not held by the publisher.

The information herein is offered for informational purposes solely, and is universal as so. The presentation of the information is without contract or any type of guarantee assurance.

The trademarks that are used are without any consent, and the publication of the trademark is without permission or backing by the trademark owner. All trademarks and brands within this book are for clarifying purposes only and are the owned by the owners themselves, not affiliated with this document.

Chapter 1: Is Your Husband / Boyfriend Controlling?

Awareness is the first step in solving any problem. The point here is that it is totally possible to be with a controlling partner, without ever actually realizing it. This will often land you in more serious trouble. Recognizing that there is something wrong with the relationship, and that it is being brought about by the controlling behavior of your boyfriend or husband, is the first step in coming up with the right solution.

Now, how do you know the difference between a dominant partner and one with a worrying controlling character? A partner who is controlling can make you feel confused, and suffocated. However, if you were once the happy, career-driven, free lady who regularly hung out with friends and enjoyed doing the things you liked, and suddenly you now feel clueless, trapped, or held back, this should make you look deeper.

A controlling spouse or boyfriend can exert power over you without you, or them, knowing about it. Is it enough to say that they are controlling if they establish boundaries, or tell you what to do, or worse, how you should feel or act? You may see it as plain dominance and decide to work on the relationship in an even more loving way, hoping your partner will somehow change. However, this can be a slippery slope. You may end up dealing with the misery for years, until it becomes too late to reverse the issue. So, the earlier you detect the signs, the quicker you can learn to deal with your partner's behaviors in a more effective and loving way. Also, you can guard yourself from the potential dangers of an abusive relationship.

Recognizing the Key Signs

A controlling man will exhibit certain signs that will help to assure you that there really is a problem. To get a wide grasp of this controlling behavior, it is wise to know the two key characteristics of controlling individuals.

Primarily, controlling men are characterized by single-mindedness. They will often assume the same mood as you. If you become angry, your partner will begin the controlling act by arguing and avoiding and even abusing you, even if simply through passive mental, or emotional abuse. This is very typical behavior for controlling people.

The second typical characteristic is if he starts to define you. This can happen if your partner constantly tells you what you feel or think. They may define you according to an image that is ideal, which lacks authenticity. What you actually think and feel can be replaced by your partner's definition. This definition generates some kind of fantasy that will pull you back towards their perfect character. This sign can be best seen through the following example scenarios:

- If you say, "I'm craving a big juicy rib eye steak, let's go to the Steakhouse around the corner for dinner," your partner might say, "No, you don't want that, it will make your stomach hurt later. You would be happier if we cooked fish at home tonight."

- If you say, "I am really trying to get into this TV series, but I'm just not hooked yet." your partner could say, "No, you aren't even trying to enjoy it!"

- If you laugh at a joke your friend made about farting, then when you get home your partner might say "I can't believe you laughed at that guy's joke. You don't even like bathroom humor – you think it's gross."

Though these are only examples, you can see how a controlling partner can attempt to define you and, at the same time, wipe out your authenticity. A controlling partner typically molds you to the ideal image in his mind. In short, controllers tend to end up with the exact opposite of what they wish to achieve.

The Other Signs

Additional signs that may denote a controlling streak are as follows:

- A controlling husband/boyfriend exhibits extreme jealousy when you show interest in other people. This means that the perfect image is really not centered on him.

- He belittles you and tries to damage your authenticity.

- He usually objects to your ideas and opinions about parenting, or other important decision-making factors.

- He makes you feel accountable, even for petty amounts of money.

- He abuses you in different ways: physical, psychological, verbal.

- He states after rage episodes that he will change, but this does not happen.

- He blames other people for his anger and bad behavior.

- He does not listen to your thoughts on future plans.

- He isolates you from your family, friends and the people around you.

- He showers you with gifts to make you totally dependent on him.

- He seems to live in a fantasy world, brought about by being too close-minded.

- He often expresses discontent at your responses to something he says or asks, and proceeds to describe how you *should have* responded instead.

If you notice these signs in your partner, action should be taken right away to achieve that intimacy, and level of equality and respect, that must be present in any relationship. It is impossible to be intimate with a controlling partner. Intimacy is a situation in which where the two persons involved understand each other and have a genuine connection. It should be known that it is impossible for controlling men to become intimate. Something first has to be done to curb or eliminate his controlling tendencies.

If you see these signs in your loved one, make sure that you help him see reality again through the proper coping techniques. He may recover, and both of you could have a better relationship. You will never know until you attempt to make changes in how you deal with your partner.

Chapter 2: Controlling Relationship: Work On It, Or Leave?

At this point in the book, you most likely have recognized that you are in a controlling relationship, or you probably would have stopped reading already. There is no need to waste time at this point. Early on, you need to make some decisions and take action, without delay. Should you choose to stay and deal with it? Or just leave your partner when things get too extreme? The decision will really depend on your circumstances. Deciding to remain in the relationship, to talk things over, is a big decision, and may take some work to get back to a point of mutual respect and intimacy. If this is what you want, there are several things that need to be done.

First, you need to have a deeper sense of self-understanding. Keep in mind that there is no one that understands how you feel and think better than yourself. No one in this world can define you. It is essential that you have a concrete self understanding and belief about the things that your husband or boyfriend is trying to tell you. If you want to eat steak, feel confident about it. If the joke was truly funny to you in your gut, don't feel bad about it – it's who you are.

Secondly, you should learn to determine whether your partner is already penetrating your boundaries. This should come at the same time as step number one. Identifying the things that your partner does to define who you are is vital. This will help you strengthen your self-belief when you are being controlled. Although you are the victim of his controlling behavior, you are totally responsible for your response, and it's not okay to let somebody walk all over you and strip you of your authenticity.

If you really want to fix things, the third step you need to take is to talk about things and force the issue. Speaking up will break the image that your partner has for you. But remember NOT to argue with a controlling partner, as this may complicate things, and set back your effort to create change. An ineffective argument with a controlling partner may appear like this:

- You: "I've decided that I want to go back to work again. I don't like being a stay-at-home mom."

- Partner: "You don't know what you want. You didn't even like your job."

- You: "You know what; I really do want to work again. I want to pursue my career as a fashion designer."

- Partner: "You don't even like fashion, or the women who work in that type of industry. Just stick to what you are doing right now."

- You: "No – I really do like designing clothes and I've been reading fashion magazines every day, and now I want to be a part of creating the trends. The women are nice, I even met the owner of the boutique down the street, and she's looking for a new designer. I really want to apply!"

- Partner: "Give me those damn magazines, so I can rip them up. You have a totally distorted view of that type of work."

Again, it is not a good idea to argue with a controller. You won't win, and he probably will never agree with you, or even be respectful of your position or viewpoint. Instead, with all the calmness that you can muster, try responding differently, by asking questions, or by simply refusing to argue or accept his portrayal of what you want/like such as this:

- You: "I've decided that I want to go back to work again. I don't like being a stay-at-home mom."

- Partner: "You don't know what you want. You didn't even like your job."

- You: "What?"

- Partner: "I said 'You don't know what you want.' Remember how much you hated your last job?"

- You: "I disagree. And contrary to what you just said, I DO know what I want, and I don't appreciate you telling me what I think, feel, or want."

- Partner: "No you don't. You don't have a clue."

- You: *STOP RESPONDING HERE. DO NOT ARGUE FURTHER.* You've done your best, expressed your perspective, and have directly refuted him once. As expected, he had to get the last word in, and didn't respect your final statement. Just remember, any further down this road, and you will regret having taken his bait.

This may seem petty, but it is the difference between getting into a pointless, mechanical argument, giving your partner the opportunity to control you, and taking control yourself.

Just a warning, do not create a heated argument if you feel that your husband or boyfriend has the potential to go into a fury. Above all things, you have to look after yourself and your children if any. Be very cautious when you deal with a controlling partner, as they will fight to realize their reality. Any threat to what they think and feel is real is recognized as an extreme problem.

Given the arguments and dialogues above, you have to know that a single conversation will not change your husband or boyfriend. But it will start to make a different within yourself, and the way you perceive your own resolve and self-esteem.

The realization on his part, on the other hand, that he's trying to control you is the beginning of healing. A few more conversations like these (that end with the same calm yet firm statement about how you don't appreciate him telling you what you feel/think/want) is exactly what's needed, repeatedly, to make sure your partner starts to see their own controlling tendencies. Change will come easiest if he realizes this way, as opposed to some sort of "stop controlling me" intervention or confrontation.

Although it is possible to stay in a controlling relationship, your main purpose should be to transform the situation, which will be discussed further in the following chapter. If you are only staying because you are totally charmed by your partner, feel helpless or consider that you don't deserve any better, then you should reassess your thoughts and feelings, and work on your own self-esteem and self-image.

Should You Leave?

If you are still miserable after trying to reverse the course of things for some time, maybe it is time to leave your controlling relationship. However, you must be clear of this in your mind. Your partner's controlling behavior could weaken as they realize that this is a decision you have made, but this does not mean that they will really change for the long-term. The important thing here is to make them recognize what their demeanor did to both you and them.

You should not feel helpless when you choose this path. If you are living with your partner, you always have the option of staying with friends and other family members. And as a last resort, shelters are always available for those who suffer from controlling spouses, willing and ready to help you. If the situation is getting too intense and dangerous, go ahead and call the police. You should not let this thing compromise your happiness and safety, nor that of your children, if you have any. So do something.

Furthermore, it is important to realize that children who are witness to a controlling relationship can be affected by this experience. If you have kids, they will require proper guidance and assistance, or they may end up being controlling as well as they advance in life, or they may believe that this behavior is natural, and therefore may not stand up for themselves if ever controlled by their own future spouse or relationship partner. Also, if their primary needs are not met, they will have the tendency to run away to a fake reality, where those needs are filled.

So, leaving your partner may well be a reasonable last resort once all other measures have been exercised. Control cycles may go on, or even become worse unless you courageously deal with your partner and what makes them control you. We'll touch on the best way to end a controlling relationship in the next chapters, as well as the best ways of working with a controlling partner. Read on for these best measures.

Chapter 3: Different Ways to Deal with and Transform a Controlling Husband / Boyfriend

Dealing with a controlling partner isn't easy. Even still, you shouldn't get totally blinded by love, or give up on taking action because it seems too difficult. You don't deserve bad treatment. If your partner acts in this way towards you then they will certainly have issues that need to be dealt with, and not tolerated. For some people, coping with the situation triumphantly may seem impossible. However, if you persevere, and do the correct things, you may be surprised by the outcome.

In dealing with a controlling partner, it is important to understand that controllers come in different shapes and sizes, and there will be multiple types of control mechanism in any person. So, with that in mind, here are some categories, and tips for dealing with your husband/boyfriend's controlling behaviors:

The Defender

Your partner may not know or admit it, but he can be over-protective a lot of the time. As far as he is concerned, he is only looking after you, or the family.

This leads to behaviors that are bossy, controlling and possessive. Although his intentions are good, they do not justify his pushing you to the limits or holding you back. The good news is that there is a good chance of transforming him. What should you do?

- Talk to Him

There is no reason to wait. There may come a time when things cannot be repaired anymore. Speak to him and let him know your feelings. Take note that men respond to logical reasoning better than when they're spoken to with openly displayed emotions. So try not to cry, shout, scream, or be dramatic in any way. Pretend you're in a professional environment, and speak calmly and in a matter-of-fact way. Make sure that you are clear as to where and when he commits his errors. If possible, provide circumstances within the past few days to help him get a better view of things.

- Be Forgiving and Open-Minded

Do not expect major changes immediately, as soon as you have laid down your points. It is possible that your partner will commit the same errors again several times. Practice patience and forgiveness each time, but make sure you lovingly point out to him these instances– this is the most vital part!

- Give a Warning

At times, your partner can become comfortable behaving in a controlling manner, not placing any effort on making changes. He should understand the severity of the circumstances, so lay your cards down. Let him know that you are serious and that, should this behavior persist, you are ready to find some temporary space or even end the relationship. When you say this, mean it.

- Last Option

When there is nothing more that can be done, if things remain the same after quite some time, separation is the last resort. This can be hard with this kind of controller, as he is not violent or enraged, but it is equally important that you should have your space in the relationship, and control over your own life. Otherwise, your self-esteem will become damaged over time, and you won't be the same strong individual you once were at the beginning of the relationship. No guy is worth that sacrifice.

The One Who Doesn't Care

Control freaks usually want a slave or a doormat, rather than a good and loving wife or girlfriend. If your partner falls into this category, there is at best a slim chance of transforming him. These men can be hard-headed and do not give in easily. But this does not mean that your case is hopeless. These things will help you deal with a partner of this kind:

- Be Unwavering

Your partner can only control you until you make a stand. So, when he pushes you to do things like run errands, simply say, "No". Stay calm and explain why you should not be doing all the work. If you become angry, he will have more reasons to exhibit unruly behavior, so be strong in your resolve to speak calmly and not become emotional. When you refuse to do something, or to answer his unnecessary inquiries, do it bluntly. He will almost certainly retaliate, but don't give in. Wait for days or weeks as he gets used to this kind of treatment. Eventually, he will either gain more rational expectations and boundaries, or he will decide to find someone else to control. You are absolutely the winner in either scenario.

- Do Not Please Him

In his mind, you are not good for anything. Therefore, there is no sense in attempting to gain his appreciation or approval by cooking, cleaning, or doing whatever it is that he so badly wants to make you do. It will not motivate him to change. Instead, try not to act inferior, but insist with your actions that you are equals. Acting inferior or giving in will only boost his ego and make the problem even worse because you just taught him that he can get what he wants by behaving that way.

The Man in Camouflage

Your man may seem gentle, loving and sweet. You may not even remember him arguing or shouting. When you disagree on things, he is always the cool one, but appears more sensible, just to put you down. This can be an absolute disguise.

He is the one who causes the argument, but behaves nobler, acting disturbed by your harsh or emotional demeanor. He says things like how he totally trusts you, but then does things that prove otherwise. To deal with this behavior, you can do the following, should you wish to remain with this man:

- Master the Game
Try your best to remain composed and calm when you are having an argument. Reject his points by responding in one short sentence or a few words. This will give him nothing or little with which to continue the argument. You'll have to act very calm, as if nothing he does or says actually gets under your skin at all.

- Give One Last Chance
Men who are good at disguising their bad side can also easily become philanderers. Simple to say, these are the kind who regularly commit adultery, but can

cover it up easily because of their clever and controlling behavior. The way out can seem cloudy if you have this type of partner. To best handle the situation, work up your emotional strength, then give him one last chance to change his ways, and if he doesn't, walk out of the relationship and never look back.

<u>The Boss by Religion</u>

These types of controlling men can often be made to see that they are being irrational and demanding, tracing it back to selfishness. However, there are those men from particular religion sects or cultures who were raised believing that women are there to simply give birth and perform chores. Their thoughts about marriage can be traced back to the Stone Age. This is not to say that all religious men fall into this category – not by any means – but you should be aware of it if you feel he is using religion or culture as an excuse to control you. If your husband feels that everything he does is absolutely perfect, or if he overestimates his contributions to the household, here is a piece of advice:

-The Solution
Transforming this type of man is next to impossible. This is because you are actually challenging his belief system, and going against the grain of his entire

world-view. Since the obvious solution of walking away may seem too narrow, or undesirable, you can still try talking to your partner. These men often care about you in their own way, and may be willing to work through this. However, this may not get you very far, so another alternative is counseling. This gives you a third party perspective on your relationship, and your partner may be open to listening to their take on the situation. Of course be sure to visit a male therapist, remembering that your partner currently sees himself as superior to women. Again, you can try all these, but be aware that the chances are slim. Regrettably, a difficult relationship such as this leads often leads to separation or divorce.

Chapter 4: The Role of Counseling and Psychotherapy

Feeling controlled for a long time can weaken your confidence. It can even make you feel depressed and anxious. To resolve this, your first action should be to talk to your partner, to let him know how you feel and what you think about things. There are times when the problem lies simply with your own communication, or lack thereof. Improving communication can potentially put a stop to the controlling behavior, especially if you approach the concept of communication with emotional calmness. It is also possible that his controlling behaviors stem from his own insecurity. With this in mind, assure your partner that you want to save the relationship, and that transforming the negative behavior is really crucial.

If you are feeling clueless about what to do, perhaps you feel that you need additional assistance to fix the problem, counseling is an excellent option. Talking to someone who can be trusted to objectively analyze the issue can help you and your partner regain your old relationship, free from manipulation, abuse and all the negativity. The counseling should involve both of you ideally, so as to assist you both in understanding your feelings and thoughts about the relationship, and your roles in the negative patterns.

Counseling may help you to realize why you are staying in the relationship, in spite of the situation, and also why your partner acts that way. If everything can be explained as an issue of communication, counseling and therapy can significantly help. It may help to bring the relationship towards healing, recommending ways to cope and transform your partner and the relationship completely. However, the purpose of counseling is not always toward reconciliation. There are times when counselors will actually suggest that breaking up is the best thing to do. It is also important to recognize that there may be things that you need to change, that the counselor may bring up. Be a good example or role model, by being open to the counselor's criticism and displaying willingness to change your own patterns if necessary.

In extreme cases, where all kinds of abuse are present in the controlling relationship, you as the victim are be recommended to undergo psychotherapy, in order to recuperate from the psychological effects of manipulation. However, the greater part of the psychotherapy should involve the controller/abuser, especially if you're planning on remaining in the relationship. Behaving in this way is an individual problem and should be handled by a psychological therapist.

There is always an underlying issue for a person behaving in a controlling manner. With psychotherapy, the root cause of the behavior can be identified, addressed, and eliminated. Recognizing and resolving the cause of the problem will help improve the person and deal with that area requiring resolution.

Chapter 5: Calling It Quits: Healing and Transformation

A controlling relationship can be very destructive. However, assessing the situation, dealing with it, and deciding to work things out can restore what has been lost. However, there can be circumstances where the only possible way to cope is to call the relationship off. If you can't get your husband or boyfriend to change, you can at least always walk out. This is a hard thing to do, but in some instances, it's the only way to make your better (or worse) half realize what the problem really is – him. And in the case that things become dangerous, you should prioritize safety above anything else – especially when it involves you, any children you may have, and other members of the family. Ending a controlling relationship can be accomplished in three steps.

Prepare to Call It Quits

Once you have tried all means to transform your partner, with the hope of continuing the relationship, and they still fail to change for the better, quitting is the last resort. There's no point ignoring it, and no reason to deny that you're being manipulated. Just think of the reasons why you have to leave. By walking out of a hopeless relationship, you can do the following:

- Restore your authenticity

- Start healthier relationships with your family, friends, etc.

- Elevate your self-worth

- Begin living without anxiety and fears

At this point, you need to plan the things you want to say. Ideally, breaking up should be calm and concise, leaving no space for your partner to beg, reason, or attempt to otherwise affect your decision. You might want to say things like: "This just isn't working" or "It's better to end this now", along with other brief statements regarding the details of parting ways (when you will move out, exchanging belongings from each other's medicine cabinets, etc.).

When you say these lines, make sure you are calm – there is no sense in accusing the other person or getting emotional now. This will just make him emotionally unstable too, or lose respect for you during the break up process. A bit of practice in front of the mirror, or with a friend, may also help you feel comfortable. If the situation is so bad that you don't even want to face your husband or boyfriend, writing an email or note, or calling over the phone, are the next best options. Make sure to end the relationship when the timing is right. Do not do this after a fight, or the day before his big job interview, or other abnormal circumstances.

You should also have an escape plan. Having a safe place to stay after the break up will stop you from going back, or being stranded. All your things should be packed as well, or you could seek help from friends to get all your stuff after the separation.

Most of all, ensure that your mind is prepared and that you have decided what is going to happen, and that it's for the best.

Implementing the Plan

The next step is to execute what you have planned. When you say you want to call it quits, be firm. It's a statement, not a question. Once said, there should be nothing that the other person can say or do to make you reverse your decision, and really you shouldn't care what his response is – it doesn't matter. So don't be disturbed if he becomes emotional, or if he acts like he doesn't care at all. It doesn't matter anymore. This can be hard, but just think about your reasons for leaving. Also, keep things short, avoid negotiations. Just say what you have practiced, and then leave.

As you say your final words, remember to maintain distance. Do not allow your partner to hug or touch you just to make you stay. Do not let yourself become controlled again when breaking up. In this, your partner may try to influence you using emotional tugs. He might attempt to bribe you with gifts or even say things like he will marry you or he will change. When you hear all these, just be reminded that you are leaving because you have been through all this before, and have determined once and for all that it will not work anymore.

When you walk away, do not tell your partner where you will be staying. Although he may think you will go to a friend's or parents' house, do not say anything about it. If you do, he may try to go to the place and force you to talk to him. When it's time to go, walk out and do not look back.

What Happens Next?

It is vital to prevent contact with a controlling partner once words are said and you have finally walked out of the relationship. Allowing contact, whether through calls, text, or Facebook, can only complicate things and make you feel more hurt and confused. If you really need to talk, like when you're getting your things, or for child matters, make sure you bring a friend with you and do it publicly. Cutting contacts with mutual friends for a while can also help in keeping him away from you.

Moving forward, don't think about changing your mind during this period of separation. Feeling empty inside is natural at first, but don't let the loneliness overwhelm you. Always remind yourself that you can live a good life – a better life actually – without him. This way, you can become that same person you used to be before the relationship.

Instead of mourning, spend more time with your loved ones, and have fun! They are your strongest support system. You can talk to them about the relationship, even getting confirmation on your thoughts and actions. They can help you significantly in the healing process.

Also, try to keep yourself busy as much as possible. Hang out with friends, get a hobby, pursue your desired career. Get out more often and plan activities in advance for the entire week to give you something exciting to do each day. Don't forget to do the things you have never done with your ex

Conclusion

A controlling husband or boyfriend is a very serious problem. Often the warning signs appear early, but tend to be neglected. This can lead things to get worse over time.

The biggest step towards ending this, enabling you to put your relationship on equal footing, is to admit that there really is a problem. Whether physical abuse is present or not, you should focus on how the relationship is making you feel about yourself. Remember, psychological and emotional abuse can have even more marked and lasting effects than physical violence.

There is no reason to endure a controlling relationship for long, as there are a lot of ways to change things for the better, many of which are found in this book. Hopefully you now realize that coping with and transforming a controlling husband/boyfriend is never impossible.

As long as you admit that there is a problem, take appropriate action, and perhaps even seek professional help, this kind of relationship will no longer have any hold over your life.

Thanks for purchasing this book! If you enjoyed it or found it helpful, please take a moment to leave a review on Amazon – that would be much appreciated!

Printed in Great Britain
by Amazon